Stories of Canada

Mapping the Wilderness

The Story of David Thompson

by

Tom Shardlow

Illustrations by Chrissie Wysotski

Series editor: Allister Thompson

Napoleon Publishing

Napoleon Publishing
Toronto Ontario Canada

Le Conseil des Arts | The Canada Cou
du Canada | for the Arts

Napoleon Publishing acknowledges the support of the Canada Council for our publishing program.

Printed in Canada

10 09 08 07 06   5 4 3 2 1

Library and Archives Canada Cataloguing in Publication

Shardlow, Tom (Thomas Frost), date-
        Mapping the wilderness : the story of David Thompson / Tom Shardlow.

Includes bibliographical references and index.
ISBN 0-929141-85-7 (bound)

        1. Thompson, David, 1770-1857--Juvenile literature.   2. Surveyors--Canada--Biography--Juvenile literature.   3. Cartographers--Canada--Biography--Juvenile literature.   I. Title.
TA533.T56S43 2006   526.9'092   C2006-903890-2

For Erin and Brianne,
always wanting another story

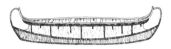

An Unmarked Grave

NO PORTRAIT

No portrait of David Thompson was ever made during his lifetime. Some say he looked like John Bunyan, the famous English preacher. Others say he looked like John Philpot Curran, the Irish orator. Still others have shown him looking exactly like Simon Fraser, the explorer and adventurer after whom the Fraser River is named.

When David Thompson's body was buried in 1857, no one marked his grave. Few people knew anything about the eighty-seven-year-old man, except that he was poor and had been selling his clothes and some old surveying instruments to buy food. Some said he had left behind a half-Indian wife. Three months later, penniless and alone, his Métis wife Charlotte also died. She was buried next to her husband of sixty years. Charlotte's grave was also unmarked.

It wasn't until 1915, after a Canadian government geologist named Joseph Tyrell uncovered and published the old man's journal, that a small monument was erected at Thompson's grave in Mount Royal Cemetery, Montreal. It reads: "DAVID THOMPSON 1770-1857. TO THE MEMORY OF THE GREATEST OF CANADIAN GEOGRAPHERS WHO FOR 34 YEARS EXPLORED AND MAPPED THE MAIN TRAVEL ROUTES BETWEEN THE ST. LAWRENCE AND THE PACIFIC."

A Remarkable Explorer

David Thompson's epitaph only begins to tell us about this modest yet remarkable man. Few explorers in history can match the accomplishments of David Thompson. He plotted and mapped over five million square kilometres of North America west of Hudson Bay. He explored the headwaters of the Mississippi. He was first to follow and chart the Columbia River from its source to the Pacific Ocean. He discovered the Athabaska Pass through the Rocky Mountains, forged many wilderness trails and established many trading posts for the North West Company across the continent. When he retired in 1812 to finish his map, David Thompson had travelled some eighty thousand kilometres on foot, horseback and canoe and had mapped a continental area whose scale is unparalleled in human history.

A STICKLER FOR DETAILS

David Thompson's detailed information of the Canadian landscape was so complete and accurate that mapmakers were to use his observations for more than a hundred years.

Why Were His Achievements Ignored?

MODEST EXPLORERS

Unlike other explorers, Thompson was reluctant to name the places he discovered after himself. It was Simon Fraser who named the Thompson River in British Columbia after his fellow explorer. Thompson, maybe in appreciation, gave the Fraser River its name.

SIMON FRASER.

Other Canadian explorers who lived in Thompson's day became famous in their own time. Alexander Mackenzie, who followed the magnificent Mackenzie River to the Arctic Ocean and who was the first to travel overland to the Pacific in 1793, was knighted by King George III. Simon Fraser, who explored the Peace River, established the first trading post in British Columbia and who was the first to map and follow the mighty Fraser River to the Pacific Ocean in 1808, was a living legend. Why were David Thompson's achievements ignored for so long?

Some say it was because he deserted the Hudson's Bay Company and joined with their rival, the North West Company. Others say it was because he needlessly delayed exploring the Columbia River to the Pacific which allowed the United States, instead of Canada, to claim the rich Columbia territory. After so many years, the truth of these allegations is hard to know. But today these criticisms seem like drops in the ocean when compared to his achievements.

GREY COAT SCHOOL

Grey Coat Charity School was chartered in 1706 by Queen Anne as part of a social experiment. In those days, poor or orphaned children were neglected and had to beg or steal in London's squalid streets as their only way of finding food and shelter. The school's founders believed that religion and education could save London's orphan boys from a life of begging and thieving.

Although the boys were housed, fed, and given grey clothes to wear, life at the school was sometimes very hard. At one point the boys revolted against the terrible treatment they were given. They rioted and threw hot coals from a fire at their cruel masters.

Nevertheless, the school did shelter and educate many orphans.

Arriving In
The New World

On the afternoon of September 2nd, 1784, David Thompson walked down the gang plank of the Hudson's Bay Company ship *Prince Rupert* and stepped onto the western shore of Hudson Bay. He was fourteen years old and had landed at Churchill Factory, the Hudson's Bay Company company post in Rupert's Land. He was thankful to have survived the turbulent seas and treacherous icebergs of the North Atlantic, but he was not happy. He had trained to be a midshipman or a junior navigator. He had hoped to enter the Royal Navy or to join a merchant ship, but instead he was beginning a seven year term as a fur trading apprentice to the Hudson's Bay Company (HBC).

An HBC advertisement designed to attract workers

Some students not only learned to read and write, but also were taught about mathematics, astronomy and navigation. These students were the lucky ones. When they left the school, they were able to help navigate sailing ships for the navy or for merchant ships.

David had received a remarkable education from an orphanage. London's Grey Coat Charity School for Boys had taught him how to navigate a ship by the stars and how to understand the ebb and flow of ocean tides. But England was not at war in 1784, so the navy was not recruiting. When the HBC approached the school asking for senior boys skilled in mathematics, Grey Coat had only two, David Thompson and Samuel McPherson. McPherson ran away rather than face the uncertain life of an HBC apprentice.

An Orphan

CHEAP GIN

In some of London's poorer districts like Whitechapel or St. Giles, David would have had difficulty finding anyone sober. Watered down wine, beer and poorly distilled gin were often bought in place of food. In St. Giles, one in every four houses was a ginshop. They were open to anyone of any age, and David would have seen men, women and children drink themselves into a stupor.

In eighteenth century society, alcohol was used by nearly everyone. Doctors often prescribed spirits or alcohol for sick patients. They thought it thinned the blood when it was too thick. It warmed the intestines and aided in digestion. They wrongly believed that liquor prevented the flu and helped cured depression. To the poor masses of London's crowded and dirty districts, alcohol was an escape. But to David, alcohol was a curse.

David was born on April 30, 1770 and was given to an orphanage at age seven. His father had died when David was two. His mother was poor and unable to provide for both David and his younger brother. His mother's choice turned out to be a wise one. Being a poor and fatherless boy in London was usually a sentence to misery. London's poor districts were crowded, dirty and crime ridden. Poverty was made worse by an abundance of cheap alcohol, usually gin called "kill grief". Seeing the devastating effect of "kill grief" on London's poor people affected David for life. He would never use alcohol, and as a fur trader in later life even refused to sell it to native peoples.

This famous illustration, "Gin Lane" by eighteenth century artist William Hogarth, shows the effects of alcohol on the poor.

An Encounter
With Smugglers

English ships in
the New World

After he was given into apprenticeship with the HBC, David boarded the *Prince Rupert* at her mooring in the Thames River in London. In May of 1784, his ship lowered her sails and made its way northward in the English Channel toward the North Sea. Not far into the Channel, a small Dutch lugger sailed alongside and offered to sell the *Prince Rupert*'s crew contraband gin. The crew had no stock of liquor, because the prices were high in London, so they bought a whole caseload at a good price from the Dutch captain. Later, when they uncorked the bottles, they spat out the "gin". All the bottles contained seawater. The Dutch smugglers had cheated them.

Captain Tunstall, master of the *Prince Rupert*, calmed his crew by reminding them they would soon be sighting the Orkney Islands off Scotland's north coast. Here they would find their precious liquor from the reliable supply smuggled off Dutch ships into Stromness port.

Prince Rupert

Prince Rupert reading the HBC charter at the founding of the company in 1670

The *Nonsuch* and the *Prince Rupert*

The *Prince Rupert* was a well-known Hudson's Bay Company ship, but the most famous HBC ship was the *Nonsuch*. King Charles II of England gave his cousin, Prince Rupert, a gift of unexplored land in the New World. Prince Rupert had asked for the gift after two French fur traders, named Radisson and Groseilliers, had told him about the furs and copper riches that they had found on the rivers draining into Hudson Bay.

The Prince borrowed some money and, with the help of some adventuresome friends, sent the first trading ship into Hudson Bay. That ship was the *Nonsuch.* The voyage of the *Nonsuch* was successful, and the Prince and his adventurous friends formed a company in 1670 called "The Company of Adventurers trading into Hudson's Bay". This name was later shortened to the Hudson's Bay Company. They named the new land Rupert's Land.

Neither King Charles nor Prince Rupert ever knew how big Rupert's Land was. The King had given his cousin all the land whose streams drain into Hudson Bay. Rupert's Land turned out to be over 3.8 million square kilometres, or almost half the size of present-day Canada. The Hudson's Bay Company is still operating today and is one of the oldest companies in the world.

A Well Travelled Route

THE ORKNEYS: GOOD WATER AND BETTER MEN

In the remote Orkney Islands of Scotland, there is a well with sweet, clean water. Known as Login's Well, it is located in the town of Stromness. The well is famous not just because of its good-tasting water, but because many renowned captains and commanders have stopped there to use it. Henry Hudson, the famous navigator who had Hudson Bay named after him, had used Login's Well more than a hundred years before Thompson's voyage. The legendary Captain Cook filled his ships with water from the well. Almost a hundred years after Thompson, Sir John Franklin topped up his barrels on his ill-fated expedition to the Arctic.

The well water was important, but something even more valuable was taken aboard at Stromness: the rugged men of Orkney. These tough islanders, used to hardships and cold weather, were suited for the hard life in the New World. Orkney Islanders made up three of every four men working in the fur trade for the HBC.

Thompson's ship was following a well travelled route. Most ships, and all HBC ships bound for the New World, stopped at Stromness, a port in the Orkney Islands. Here they took on water, supplies and additional men. From Stromness, the winds filled the *Prince Rupert*'s sails and carried it along the 59th parallel of latitude past Greenland's icebergs and into Hudson Bay.

It must have been a difficult voyage for David. Although he had the skills to help guide the *Prince Rupert* on her icy passage, he knew now that, as an apprentice to the HBC, he would never be given a chance to navigate a ship across the open ocean.

Orkney Islands

SCOTLAND

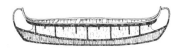

Life At Churchill Factory

David's ship had arrived at Churchill Factory, where it was officially join join the HBC. When the *Prince Rupert* left Churchill to return to England, David's heart sank. He wrote in his journal: "While the ship remained at anchor, my parent and friends appeared only a few weeks' distance, but when the ship sailed and from the top of the rocks I lost sight of her, the distance became immeasurable, and I bid a long and sad farewell to my noble, my sacred country, an exile forever."

Life at Churchill Factory did nothing to cheer him up. Most of David's time, as apprentice clerk, was spent making entries into the HBC account books. The rest of the time he was employed in the endless job of gathering firewood. When winter came, he was holed up in a frozen bunkhouse.

Wood was always hard to find at Churchill. The apprentices were allowed to light only one fire in the morning and one at night to keep warm. The rest of the time they had no heat. It was so cold that ten centimetres of ice formed on the inside walls of their bunkhouse. When spring finally came, the warm weather brought its own problems. Mosquitoes and blackflies tormented everyone day and night.

MOSQUITOES

The plague of mosquitoes and blackflies at Churchill was so bad that the HBC men tried everything to keep them off. They smeared oil and tar on their skin. They stood over smoking fires. They piled on extra layers of clothes but nothing could keep the bugs off. Even the wildlife suffered and could not feed or stand still from constant harassment and bites.

Attacked By
The French

TODAY A PARK

The mouth of the Churchill River was a perfect location for a stone fort. The river is over half a kilometre wide, and there is a natural harbour and plenty of limestone for building. Construction began on the fort in 1732, and it took forty years to complete. The walls were 6.5 metres high and 11 metres thick, with forty cannons set along the ramparts. Today Fort Prince of Wales, the post's later name, is a national historic site.

Churchill Factory was once the site of Fort Prince of Wales. The HBC fort had been occupied for over a hundred years, but when David Thompson arrived, Fort Prince of Wales was in ruins. It had been attacked and plundered two years earlier by the French, who were at war with England. La Pérouse, the French commander, had taken eight thousand beaver and four thousand marten skins from the fort's storehouse. This plunder was worth a fortune. The commander was lenient with the Hudson's Bay men and returned them unharmed to England for ransom.

Churchill
Factory

A Clerk's Life

SELLING PELTS

Money was not used in the fur trade. Instead trade items were sold by comparing their value to beaver pelts according to guidelines set in London. A prime beaver pelt was called a made beaver (MB) and it could buy, for example, one brass kettle. Surprisingly, it took six MB to buy one pound of porcelain beads, while a wool blanket cost seven MB. Other furs besides beaver were traded, but all furs were compared to the beaver standard. It took six muskrat skins, for example, to equal one MB, but one black fox was worth three MB.

The factor often adjusted the London rules so he could make a personal profit. If London wanted one MB for a brass kettle, the Factor would ask and get three MB. The extra two were his profit.

Life as a trading clerk for David meant joyless hours of stocking storeroom shelves, carefully writing entries in the company's ledger, and stowing furs for pressing and shipping. Senior Company traders would grade the pelts of animals like muskrat, fox and beaver brought to the post by Chipewyan trappers. The pelts were exchanged for desirable items like blankets, copper kettles, knives and gun powder.

David's job was to fetch the items from the storeroom, stow the furs and record the daily exchange of goods. The traders followed strict trading rules, set by London and the factor (who was in charge of the post), on how much to give for each type of fur brought in.

Learning To Hunt

"...I was educated...a scholar who had a mathematical education... For all I have seen in [the company's] service neither writing or reading was required," wrote David in his journal. Fortunately, Mr. Hodges, the company surgeon, and Mr. Prince, captain of a trading sloop, took David under their wing. They lent him books and taught him how to hunt and shoot ptarmigan and other wildfowl.

Eventually David became an expert marksman and hunter. These skills were as equally important as reading and writing when travelling long distances through unexplored wilderness.

FOOD

Some cattle were brought from Britain to provide beef for the main trading posts, but much of the fur trader's meat came from fish and wildlife. Caribou were hunted on the tundra. Moose taken in the woodlands and buffalo from the grasslands provided a large part of a trader's diet. Small animals too, like muskrat and beaver, were eaten.

Canada's National Animal

An 1844 illustration of beavers

Rodents are a group of animals that include mice, rats and squirrels, but the largest rodent in North America is the beaver. Adult beavers weigh from fourteen to forty-five kilograms and can measure over one metre from nose to tail. They have a large flat tail and webbed feet to help them swim. Their large front teeth (incisors) are used to chew tree bark, their favourite food. At night, beavers chew right through the trunks of trees. When the tree falls, they drag its branches to the water to store as food for the winter.

Beavers also use branches and mud to build dams and make homes for themselves. The dams are about one metre tall and fifteen to sixty metres long. Behind the dam is a pond. The beavers build their home, called a lodge, in the pond. For safety, they put their lodge entrance underwater. Most important, beavers have beautiful chestnut brown fur that is soft and thick. This fur could be sold for high prices and is the main reason Europeans explored and settled Canada in the early years, and the reason that the beaver is Canada's national animal.

SAMUEL HEARNE

Samuel Hearne's 5600 kilometre exploration to the Arctic Ocean proved there was no Northwest Passage to the Pacific Ocean out of Hudson Bay. But his findings were mostly ignored, and explorations from Hudson Bay to discover the passage continued. Hearne was only given a small bonus for his troubles. He wrote about his explorations in his journal, then returned to England in 1787. He died two years later at the age of forty-eight.

Samuel Hearne in the Arctic

His First Boss

Samuel Hearne was in charge of Fort Prince of Wales when David Thompson arrived. The person in charge of a HBC post was called the factor, which is why trading posts were called factories.

Hearne was a great explorer. He had travelled to the Arctic Ocean from Fort Prince of Wales and had explored a territory the size of Russia. But later in his life, after his surrender of the fort to the French, he became depressed.

Hearne's wife had starved to death, and his close friend, Chief Matonabbee, had hanged himself after La Pérouse, the French commander, took the factor and his men as captives to England in 1783.

Samuel Hearne must have treated his new apprentice, David Thompson, badly, because Thompson disliked the factor for the rest of his life. Maybe it was because when David was transferred, Hearne sent him, without adequate supplies, on a two hundred and forty kilometre walk to his new post at York Factory. Thompson was given only a blanket and a small amount of food for the journey. The two native guides, provided by the factory, were supplied with so much alcohol that they were drunk and unable to travel for many days at a time.

David's Second Boss

NORTH WEST COMPANY

In 1779 there were many small fur trading companies competing with the Hudson's Bay Company for furs. These independent traders were mostly Scottish, but they employed rugged French-Canadian canoemen called voyageurs to trade with the natives. The voyageurs travelled far inland by canoe instead of waiting for the natives to bring the furs to established forts. Soon, however, it became hard for the small traders to make a profit. The natives were able to drive up fur prices by selling furs to the highest bidder. Simon McTavish, one of the wily Scottish traders, organized all the small independent traders into a cooperative group. The group shared their trade goods and money and divided the profits among themselves. This stopped the competition and squabbling among them. They called themselves the North West Company.

Simon McTavish,
founder of the NWC

York Factory, like Churchill, was a major trading depot, where ships from England off-loaded trade goods and took on bundles of fur. It was a busy place, and David's life at York Factory was not much different from his life at Churchill except for two things. The young apprentice was given more time to learn how to hunt and fish than at Churchill. He was taught how to snare snowshoe hares using brass wire and how to trap grouse in a fish net. He learned how to catch fish baiting his hook with the heart of a grouse.

But more importantly, the energetic factor, Humphrey Martin, was impressed with David and decided to send him inland to help establish new trading posts. Up until now, the HBC had mostly relied on natives to bring furs to the factories on the shores of Hudson Bay. The North West Company, however, was building trading posts inland on the western plains. The new company was buying the furs before they got to the HBC factories on the coast.

His First Brigade

BIRCH BARK CANOES

Birch bark canoes were made entirely from materials gathered in the forest. Bark was carefully peeled off the trunks of birch trees. Cedar wood was split and carved for the gunnels and ribs. Thin roots were dug, and pitch, a thick gummy substance, was scraped from spruce trees. Stones from a fire heated water. The bark, split wood and roots were soaked in hot water to make them pliable. The softened bark was bent over the cedar ribs and lashed to the side of the boat with spruce roots. The stern and bow were sewn up, and every stitch and hole was gummed over with pitch. A supply of pitch, bark and ribs was taken along to make repairs, which were needed quite often to keep the canoe afloat.

David was assigned to one of twelve canoes in a brigade that was sent west by Humphrey Martin to build a new fort on the Saskatchewan River. The HBC needed inland posts to compete with those being built by the North West Company. David helped load each of the canoes with six ninety-pound bundles of trade goods.

In the months ahead, he learned to paddle, line and portage the light birch bark craft along wilderness waterways. He took his turn pulling the canoe upstream by a line attached to its bow. He waded knee deep in the cold water with the line tight over his shoulder. The others pushed and shoved the soft bark hull, guiding it between rocks and around root wads. This work might go on for weeks at a time until the canoe could be paddled again.

Tough Portages

Portaging was the most difficult job on the fur brigades. It happened when the brigade came to a place where they had to carry the cargo and canoes over land to another waterway.

David hoisted heavy bales on his back and slung a trump line across his forehead to help steady the load. He staggered along root-strewn trails until he could unload the cargo at the next river or lake. Finally, the canoes were shouldered on the men's backs and were portaged over land.

At night the canoes became shelters. They were overturned on the shore, and the men slept underneath them.

PORTAGE

Portage is a French word meaning carrying. Each portage or place where the canoes had to be carried was different. Some took only a few minutes to cross from one waterway to the next, while others took weeks of hard slogging.

One famous portage was called Grand Portage. It was a nine mile trail from Lake Superior to rivers that flowed to the Arctic Ocean and Hudson Bay.

MURDEROUS COMPETITION

In the beginning, the NWC and HBC men at distant posts were friendly and helped each other. As the years went by, however, competition between them became murderous. Fur traders from one company would shoot men paddling the canoes of the other company. Posts were burned in winter, leaving the unfortunate inhabitants to face death by starvation.

Eventually, in 1812, warfare broke out at the Red River Colony where Lord Selkirk's HBC settlers fought against NWC hunters and traders. Nineteen HBC settlers and one NWC man were killed in what became known as the Battle of Seven Oaks.

The Battle of Seven Oaks

Following The River

David's brigade, like many earlier brigades, followed the Saskatchewan River westward. It was the fur trader's highway across the plains. He fell in love with the river as it meandered under an expansive blue sky. Sweet smelling poplar trees and shimmering aspens lined the river's bank. Above the river, low-lying hills rolled gently away like waves on a vast ocean.

It was only a month since David had left York Factory, but he knew he felt more at home in this new wild place than any other place he had known. The brigade stopped at their trading post at Cumberland House just long enough to take on fresh supplies. They needed to push on if they were going to have time to set up a new post before winter set in.

The brigade split up where the Saskatchewan River forked into the north and south branches. David went with four canoes to follow the south branch into new territory. They were only a short way up the river when they came across men busy with axes constructing a log building on the bank. The men were speaking French and were dressed in bright-coloured hats and grey blanket coats. These men were called *Canadiens* and they were building a post for the NWC. David's brigade beached their canoes just upstream and began to build a competing HBC post. The new trading post was named South Branch House.

The Cree

TRADING WITH THE PLAINS TRIBES

For some plains people in Thompson's time, trading with Europeans was still new. Some had never seen a white man. They could not believe that they could trade beaver and wolf skins for valuable items. They could buy sewing awls and strong needles to replace the troublesome thorns used to sew leather. They could make fire quickly with flint and steel instead of the old way using glowing embers. Most of all, they were able to buy guns. Guns meant easier hunting and victory over enemy tribes. Now the strongest tribes were not those with the bravest warriors or the largest numbers but the ones who had the most guns.

At South Branch House, Thompson learned about the business of trading and about the Cree. He found the Cree to be proud and independent. To David, these people and the plains tribes were tall and fine looking. He admired their leather clothes painted with red and yellow dyes. He studied their language and their culture. He saw how they used horses for hunting buffalo and observed how they fitted dogs with side bags to carry belongings or harnessed them to long poles for hauling buffalo hides. The Cree and other First Nations people showed David how to adapt and to thrive in this wild land.

This photo of a Cree chief was taken in the late nineteenth century.

PEMMICAN

Pemmican was the English spelling of the Cree word pimikan (pe-me-kan). It was made from slices of buffalo, moose, elk or deer meat dried in the hot sun or over a fire. The meat was pounded into powder between stones. Dried berries, melted fat and bone marrow grease were added to the mixture. Sometimes wild mint leaves or wild onion was added for flavour. Pemmican could be eaten plain, dissolved into soup, or added to stew. It preserved well, lasting up to four years and still tasting the same. The HBC bought tons of pemmican to feed its paddlers. One man could thrive on a pound per day of pemmican, which was equivalent to about five pounds of meat. Pemmican was bought from natives and later from Métis, whose community thrived on the pemmican production industry.

Meat drying on racks

Thompson the Fur Trader

When the HBC brigade returned east with its load of furs, Thompson was thankful that he didn't have to go all the way to York Factory. He was left behind with a few men at Cumberland House to spend the summer gathering supplies of food. He tended nets in Cumberland Lake, catching fish for smoking and rendering into lamp oil. He helped the natives make pemmican from dried buffalo meat, fat and berries. When the brigade returned that fall, David was excited to travel west again, this time to the new post at Manchester House. It was the jumping-off place for explorations further west in Peigan country.

David Thompson was one of a few hand-picked traders selected to explore the new territory. When they headed out in September of 1787, David was no longer a pale company clerk. He was a fur trader, and like the other men, he had his own trade goods and would make his own profit from them. David was now seventeen years old.

THE BLACKFOOT

The Blackfoot were a nomadic and warlike people who followed the buffalo across the grasslands of what is now Alberta and Montana. Before Europeans came, the Blackfoot hunted buffalo on foot and used dogs to carry their provisions. Legends say the Blackfoot were named for their blackened feet caused by walking across burned prairie grass.

The Blackfoot were actually made up of three tribes, the Blackfoot in the north, the Bloods in the east, and the Peigan in the west. When they acquired European guns, and later horses, the Blackfoot became very powerful warriors. They drove out other native groups like the Kootenay and Salish. Blackfoot power did not last long, however. The disappearance of the large buffalo herds, alcohol trade, and European diseases like smallpox took their toll. By the 1870s, the Blackfoot were nearly wiped out.

Today the remaining Blackfoot, Blood, and Peigan live in parts of southern Alberta and northern Montana.

Travels With A Mountain Man

Thompson's trading party was led by James Gady. Gady was a mountain man who had lived with the Peigans, and he knew their culture. He told David that these natives were different from the Chipewyan and Cree he had known.

The Peigans were warlike and belonged to a group known as the Blackfoot. They seldom trapped animals for their own use but followed the buffalo which supplied them with most of their food and clothing. For the most part, they had little contact with fur traders, Gady told him, but they wanted horses, guns and tobacco. They were willing to act as middlemen, supplying the HBC men with furs from the Kootenay and Salish people. But they would be offended and would cut off trading if Gady and his men dealt directly with the other tribes.

Into Peigan Country

NATIVE HELP

The travels of Thompson and other fur traders and explorers would have been very difficult without the help of native peoples. Thompson was rescued from death at least twice during his explorations by friendly natives. Native guides often showed the way to Europeans trekking across the continent in search of trade routes. Fur traders often married native women, who taught their husbands many lessons about how to survive in the wilderness.

David followed on foot behind Gady. Gady rode one horse and led another deep into Peigan country, but young Thompson could only afford one horse, and it was fully loaded with supplies. The party travelled twenty-four kilometres a day but found no buffalo or elk and were soon weak with hunger.

They had not gone unseen, however, and eventually a dozen well-armed Peigan scouts intercepted the trading party. Fortunately, the scouts were friendly and gave Thompson and the men a freshly killed cow buffalo for an evening feast. The next day the scouts took the traders to the main Peigan camp.

A plains native encampment

Saukamappee

The interior of a Plains native lodging

SCALPS

A scalp was a flap of skin and hair cut from an enemy's head as a trophy of war. It brought honour to the one who took it. For a scalp to have value to a Peigan warrior, it had to be taken from an enemy he himself had killed. A scalp taken from someone another had killed was worth nothing.

The Peigans believed a scalp captured the soul of those killed in battle. The scalp or soul was often given as a gift to the victor's dead ancestors who would use the scalp's soul as slaves in the afterlife.

At the Peigan camp, David and the others traded ammunition and tobacco for choice fox and beaver skins.

David was lodged with a grey-haired elder named Saukamappee. This old man and David became good friends, partly because David could speak some Cree. David and Saukamappee also shared a similar past. They had both left their home and family behind when they were just boys. Saukamappee, the Peigan word for young man, was originally a Cree who had come to live with the Peigans as a teenager.

David passed many nights listening to and learning from the old Cree warrior. He learned about tribal customs and about the terrible tribal warfare that had raged over the plains. Saukamappee himself had taken many scalps from the heads of Kootenay and Snake warriors.

INTRODUCTION OF HORSES

Horses were introduced to North America by Spanish settlers. Native peoples soon began using horses to carry their belongings when hunting buffalo and for warfare. Horses reached Canada some time in the 1770s.

The Peigans told a story of the first horse. A Kootenay man whose family was starving was forced to trade some horses to his Peigan enemy for food. The Peigans, who knew nothing of horses, thought the strange animals must have come from the sky and called them "sky dogs". At first the new owners tried to feed the horses dried meat and berries, but the animals refused to eat. Finally the horses lowered their heads and began to chew grass from the ground, to the delight of the tribesmen. Grass was plentiful and no work was needed to obtain it.

Horses became so important to the plains tribes that a tribesman's wealth was measured by the number of horses he owned.

David's Protector

From Saukamappee, David learned how the deadly disease smallpox had taken the lives of so many natives. Saukamappee and his people believed the disease was punishment from the Great Spirit for the bloody intertribal warfare that had been raging for years.

Thompson was told how the great war chief, Kootenae Appee, had taken his warriors as far south as California to raid horses from the Spanish. He learned that Kootenae Appee planned battle strategies that defeated much stronger enemies by using ambushes and fighting retreats.

Fortunately for David, the great chief had, at

the request of Saukamappee, agreed to protect Thompson while in Peigan lands. The young fur trader was very impressed when he finally met Kootenae Appee, and they became friends.

A Turning Point

FIREWOOD

Collecting, cutting and stacking firewood occupied a large part of the daily life at a trading post. After a few winters, most of the trees near a post had been cut and burned for fuel. An abundant supply of good firewood was important when selecting where a post would be located.

David felt fortunate not to have to return east for the winter. Instead, he was stationed at Manchester House after his very successful trading mission among the Peigans. Thompson, Gady and the other men had returned with a fine take of prime beaver.

Now David's job was to care for the company horses and collect firewood for the long winter. But in December, just days before Christmas, his life took a major turn. While collecting firewood, he slipped in the snow, fell down a bank and broke his leg. It was a bad break, and he was forced to spend the rest of winter in bed.

Near Death

NO REAL DOCTORS

In Thompson's day, if you broke a bone, it often meant suffering from a lifelong deformity. Few in the wilderness knew how to properly set a broken bone. Even those who were assigned the job of surgeon might actually have been butchers, whose knowledge of human anatomy came from cutting up animals.

Still unable to walk in the spring, the young invalid was canoed downriver to Cumberland House. He was left in the care of two HBC men at the now inactive post. They had little idea of how to care for him, and in time he became thin and very weak. He was discovered near death by a kind-hearted Cree woman.

Using berries and healing herbs, she slowly nursed him back to life, but his future as a fur trader looked bleak. His leg was still unusable, and as the next winter approached, he had to face the prospect of a future as a company clerk, limping about a trading post filling out the company's accounting books.

Cumberland House

Thompson Meets An Astronomer

PHILIP TURNOR

Philip Turnor was the first surveyor employed by the HBC. He made two journeys to Rupert's Land for the purpose of map-making. On his second journey he met David Thompson and trained the young apprentice in astronomical surveying.

Turnor was a well-known man of science. He had worked with the Astronomer Royal at the Royal Observatory in Greenwich, England, recording observations of the stars. He helped compile the famous Nautical Almanac used by celestial navigators like Captain Cook to find their way across vast uncharted oceans.

Fortunately for Thompson, his life as a trading clerk didn't last long. In the fall of 1789, only two months after being assigned as clerk to Cumberland House, an unexpected visitor arrived. It was Philip Turnor, the famed HBC surveyor.

Turnor was a well-known astronomer from England whose job was to map the Athabaska country and to train some HBC men as surveyors and mapmakers. Even though David's broken leg might not heal properly, Turnor choose the young clerk as his student. Thompson's enthusiasm and his mathematical and navigation training from Grey Coat School were appreciated by the old master.

Finding His Way
By The Stars

FINDING LONGITUDE

One of the great scientific problems in Thompson's time was finding what longitude you were on when travelling on land or sea. The earth's surface is divided by imaginary lines. The lines running north and south are called longitude. Those running east to west, like the equator, are latitude. There were several methods for determining longitude, but the lunar method was the only one land explorers could use. The lunar method involved measuring the angle between the moon and certain stars. A calculation involving the difference between the angle measured where you stood and an angle at Greenwich, England listed in the Nautical Almanac gave the longitude of the traveller.

Turnor showed David how to use the travels of the moon across the night sky as a clock. He showed David how to measure the angle of Polaris, the north star, above the horizon using a sextant. But most important, Turnor instructed his student in mathematics. It took many hours of exacting calculations to plot the position of a trading post or river using latitude and longitude.

David Thompson using a sextant

Thankful For His Life

A FORGOTTEN EXPLORER

Peter Fidler has been called Canada's forgotten explorer. In 1791 Fidler was the first HBC man to reach the rich Athabaska fur country. He was the first European to trade with the Kootenay peoples of the Rocky Mountain foothills. He surveyed and mapped almost eight thousand kilometres of the western wilderness. However, it was Thompson who eventually became known as Canada's foremost mapmaker.

This giant wooden statue of Peter Fidler is a tourist attraction in Elk Point, Alberta.

That winter David helped to dig the grave of Mr. Hudson, Philip Turnor's assistant, who had died of unknown causes. David knew the grave could easily have been his own if just a few months earlier, he had not been saved by the Cree woman. He began to feel very fortunate for the events of his life. If he had not broken his leg, he might never have studied under the famous astronomer. If he had not been orphaned, he might never have learned mathematics and navigation at Grey Coat Charity School. Now, Hudson's death meant Turnor would need a new assistant.

Thompson studied many nights bent over books in dim candlelight. He wanted to be ready to become Turnor's new assistant. But he studied too long and too late into the nights. Eventually his eyes became so inflamed, he could no longer see. When Turnor left Cumberland House, he was forced to take another young man, Peter Fidler, instead of Thompson, as his new assistant.

Starting his Map-making Career

RELUCTANT TO CHANGE

Some men in the HBC felt maps had little value. These men already knew how to find their way along rivers and lakes and across portages to the next post. They had special knowledge of the trails, and if they needed help they hired native guides. They saw maps as a threat and even dangerous. With maps, anyone, including the competing North West Company, could find the fur trade trails. Fortunately for Thompson, this backward thinking was overruled by wiser men in London.

Thompson's leg and eyes eventually recovered enough for him to once again travel the fur routes. Now, however, he was on a mission. Turnor had recommended that Thompson be made surveyor to the HBC. In 1790, at age twenty, Thompson began his new career by each day plotting his position as he travelled along the unmapped fur trading trails. He was surveying to make the first map of the Muskrat Country between Reindeer Lake and Hudson Bay.

But the company kept Thompson travelling the same old routes for the next five years, and the adventuresome surveyor became bored and frustrated with his repetitive routine. He wanted to explore and map new country.

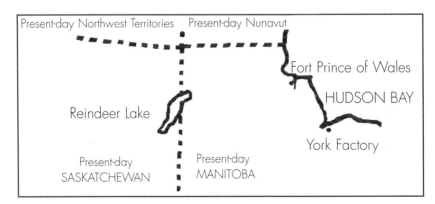

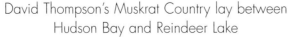

David Thompson's Muskrat Country lay between Hudson Bay and Reindeer Lake

His First Expedition

SURVIVAL KIT

Fish nets were a very good way to capture food. The nets could be folded and carried in the canoe and were much better at catching fish than a baited hook. Today some wilderness survival kits include a small gillnet.

Finally, in 1796, Thompson was sent to map a new route to the Athabaska fur district. However, some of his superiors in the company placed little value on the expedition, and he was given almost no support. Undeterred, David built his own birch bark canoe, packed a fish net and a musket in order to be able to find food on the trail, and hired two Chipewyan youths to help him.

Thompson found a new route but nearly died coming home. His canoe capsized, he lost almost all his provisions, and he severely injured his foot. With no food, Thompson and his young guides tried eating eaglets they stole from an eagles nest. It made them very sick, and only food and help from a passing band of Chipewyan saved their lives.

33

Failure

FUR COMPANIES AS EMPLOYERS

The reward for most faithful Hudson's Bay traders was promotion and finally retirement on a pension back home in Scotland or England. They usually started with a low paying apprenticeship, which bound them to seven years of service. This was followed with contracts for services for another period of years until retirement. In contrast, the NWC allowed their company men to share in the company profits and act more as free agents.

When Thompson had recovered from his first expedition, he mounted a second one to retrace his route. This time, although he had good canoes, plenty of experienced men and supplies, the expedition was forced to a standstill. Long portages and dried-up streams prevented progress, and they had to spend the winter in a makeshift hut. It was a very hard winter, with freezing temperatures at a record low. Worse still, the fur trading had been unprofitable. David Thompson's new route was abandoned. His first explorations had failed, and he was ordered back to routine fur trading duties.

The coats of arms of
left: The Hudson's Bay Company and right: The North West Company

Risking It All

Alexander
Mackenzie

**TRADE
ROUTES
TO THE WEST**

In 1793,
Alexander
Mackenzie
reached the Pacific
Ocean by travelling
overland across Canada.
He was and still is the North
West Company's best known explorer.
Thompson, along with every other fur
trader and trail blazer, knew of
Mackenzie's accomplishments. However,
the path Mackenzie found was not a
practical route to the Pacific. The
NWC would keep searching for a
usable trade route for almost another
twenty years.

David Thompson was no longer a
young apprentice. He was twenty-
seven years old, and the
company wanted him to
become an administrator. They
offered to make him "Master of
the Northward", or manager in
charge of a vast fur trading
district. But Thompson's heart
yearned for new trails and
unexplored wilderness. When the
HBC refused to let him continue
his explorations, he resigned.
On May 23rd, 1797, David
Thompson travelled alone one hundred
and twenty kilometres to the nearest North
West Bay Company post. That company
needed an experienced surveyor and
mapmaker to find new trade routes to the
west. Now they had one.

GRAND PORTAGE

Grand Portage was the nerve center of the NWC. It was strategically located on a height of land near Lake Superior. From Grand Portage, trading parties could travel west to the Saskatchewan draining into Hudson Bay or the Mackenzie, which flows to the Arctic Ocean. Eastward were the Great Lakes, the St. Lawrence and finally the Atlantic Ocean. Along these routes, trade goods and fur flowed across great distances stretching from Europe to the far reaches of the Arctic. Almost all NWC trade going in any direction passed through Grand Portage.

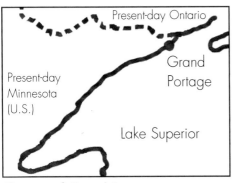

The site of Grand Portage is now part of Minnesota, in the United States

The Wrong Company?

At Grand Portage, the headquarters of the NWC, David found a rough and rowdy settlement. There were hundreds of people speaking English, French, Chipewyan and Cree and all manner of mixed trading languages in between. Sprawled outside the stockade were native birch bark lodgings and the ramshackle log huts of the traders. Hide tents and upturned canoes, sheltering the French speaking voyageurs from Montreal, were scattered along the river bank.

The busiest building inside the stockade was the cantine, where cheap rum flowed freely. Next to the cantine was the jailhouse. It too was very busy. This was not like the orderly and businesslike HBC posts David was accustomed to. He must have wondered if he had made a mistake and joined the wrong company.

The Fur Trade's
Most Famous Explorer

CLAN

Many of the senior partners in the NWC were related. Simon McTavish, the company founder put his nephew, William McGillivray, in charge of trading operations. McGillivray's brother Duncan was an expedition leader for western explorations. They relied on a group of related families called a clan and relationships from their Scottish heritage to bind the company together. Thompson was an outsider, but they needed his talents.

William McGillivray

At Grand Portage, Thompson met the NWC senior partner William McGillivray and the famous explorer Alexander Mackenzie. Thompson, like all people in the fur trade business, knew about Mackenzie's famous explorations to the Arctic and Pacific Oceans. But McGillivray and Mackenzie also knew about David Thompson and his skills as mapmaker, backwoodsman and fur trader. They were glad to have him and wouldn't waste his talent. He was exactly what they needed to expand trade and map routes into the west.

ALCOHOL

Alcohol had a devastating effect on native people. It destroyed their family life and undermined their traditional ways. Tribal elders were powerless to stop its widespread use. Some believe alcohol was the main cause for the loss of much of native culture.

Refusing To Trade Alcohol

One problem Thompson would have faced is the use of alcohol for trade. All fur traders, including the NWC and the HBC, bartered a certain amount of alcohol for furs. Alcohol, however, was the main currency of trade with the NWC.

Thompson's early life experiences, where he saw how alcohol ruined the lives of London's poor, had left him with strong convictions about its dangers. He would never use alcohol himself or trade liquor to the natives. Some natives respected him for this, and it may have saved his life later on when he was under siege by Peigan warriors.

New Assignment

DEFINING THE CANADA-UNITED STATES BORDER

After the Americans won independence from Britain in the Revolutionary War, there was a need to separate American and British territories. Finally, after long negotiations, the 49th parallel was chosen as the border to at least as far west as the Mississippi River. West, beyond the headwater of the Mississippi, there was no border. In later years, the remainder of the border to the Pacific was negotiated. David Thompson's surveys and maps played a role in those negotiations.

The NWC gave David his first assignment. They wanted him to map the exact location of their trading posts, because a new border between the British territories and the United States was expected. Many of the NWC posts in the headwaters of the Missouri and Mississippi Rivers could eventually end up in foreign territory. Thompson's assignment was to map the location of these posts, and if needed, have them closed or moved further north into British territory.

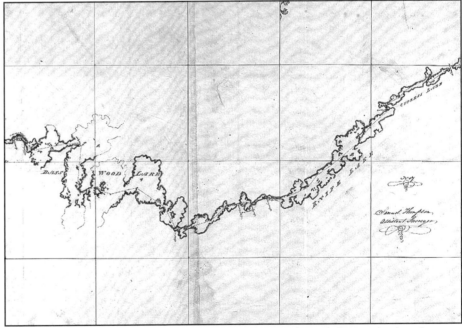

This map by David Thompson shows his work in defining the border between the United States and Canada.

Blinding Blizzards

THE MANDAN

The Mandan were a sophisticated and peaceful people. They lived in earthen houses in permanent settlements in the Upper Missouri River. They grew crops but mostly lived off trading. They traded with many other tribes including the Crow, Shoshoni and Cree. They often acted as go-betweens for native and European traders, and their trade network stretched all across the continent.

Thompson's border expedition left Grand Portage in August of 1797. He travelled west to the Qu'Appelle River then south until he reached McDonnell's House in mid winter. Unwilling to stop, he headed further south toward the Mandan country of the Upper Missouri.

It was one of the coldest winters on record, and temperatures plunged to -33° Celsius. His party, now using dog sleds, was caught in an unrelenting blizzard. Thompson, unable to see in the blinding snow, used wind direction to find his way.

When the storm finally cleared, Thompson and his men spent Christmas Day hiding in a snow bank from a Sioux war party. Finally, on December 30, they reached the safety of the Mandan villages.

A nineteenth century illustration of winter travel in Rupert's Land

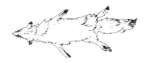

Unmatched Achievement

HEADQUARTERS MOVED

In following years, Grand Portage, the heart of NWC trading empire, was found to be south of the 49th parallel and in United States territory. The post was forced to move north and was renamed Fort William.

When Thompson returned to Grand Portage only ten months after he had departed he had surveyed nearly 6500 kilometres and located many trading posts.

He had mapped not only the headwaters of the Mississippi River but also parts of Lake Superior. It was an achievement unmatched in the history of North American exploration.

Fort William, present-day Thunder Bay, Ontario

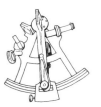

A Route To The Pacific

A FORTUNE FROM SEA OTTERS

Captain Cook's report to the British Admiralty told of valuable furs traded with the natives at Nootka. Within a few years of hearing the report, both American and British ships were heading for the Pacific Northwest. They began trading knives, axes and copper sheets for sea otter pelts. The pelts were shipped to Canton, China and traded at very high prices. In China, the ships were loaded with spices and tea. The fully-laden trading ships then sailed around Cape Horn and back to Britain or America, where they made a huge profit.

After returning from his border expedition, Thompson was sent back to the Athabaska country to bolster NWC trade. The NWC now had more competition than just the HBC. A new fur company formed by Alexander MacKenzie called the XY company was also buying furs. MacKenzie had left the NWC to become their competitor.

Thompson's setback in exploration was not to last long. William McGillivray recalled Thompson to headquarters. There he told David he wanted him to find a new route to the Pacific Ocean by crossing the Rocky Mountains. The HBC and American ships were reaping a huge profit from sea otter pelts traded from the natives of the Pacific Northwest. The pelts were shipped and sold in China.

The NWC wanted a land route to the Pacific to cash in on the lucrative new market.

Captain
James Cook

Meddling Bosses Cause Delay

JEALOUS TRIBES

Thompson knew the Kootenay regularly crossed the Rockies on horseback. His plan was to follow a band of Kootenay on their way back to their home near a river that the natives said flowed to the sea. This way he would find his pass through the Rockies and the river route to the Pacific. The Peigan, however, were jealous of the Kootenay and wanted to control all trade between Europeans and Plains tribes. They worked hard to spoil Thompson's plan by chasing off any Kootenay that came near the traders.

Duncan McGillivray, the Superintendent's brother, was put in charge of Thompson's explorations. But Duncan left Thompson behind and spent a year with his own guides trying to be first to find a new way through the Rockies. When that failed, instead of putting Thompson in charge, he left James Hughes and an unreliable Cree guide to lead the expedition. Their attempts also failed, and the exploration was called off in 1802. Left on his own, Thompson, with the help of the natives, would likely have succeeded in finding a route across the mountains.

Charlotte Small

COUNTRY WIVES

Fur traders often married native women. These women could teach their European husbands how to survive in the wilderness, how to speak native languages, and how to deal with native peoples in trade. Unfortunately, many traders, including the factors, thought of these marriages as having a second or "country wife". When it came time for the traders to return to Europe, most left their native wives and children behind. David Thompson was one of the few who remained faithful to his "country" marriage. He stayed married to Charlotte all his life, even after he returned to live in the Eastern townships. He loved her and helped her to raise their thirteen children.

Thompson was once again sent back to trade furs in the bug-invested swamp-strewn Muskrat Country. This region held little interest for him, because he had already carefully mapped it. It was here, however, that he met Charlotte Small.

Charlotte was the daughter of Patrick Small, the factor at the NWC post at Isle-a-la-Crosse, in today's central Saskatchewan. Charlotte's mother was Cree, and when the factor returned to Britain, he left his native wife and children behind.

David and Charlotte's native marriage ceremony was simple. David gave gifts to Charlotte's relatives, then in front of everyone he declared that Charlotte was now his wife.

A Tactical Error

LEWIS AND CLARK

In 1803, United States President Thomas Jefferson put in place one of his long-held ambitions, an expedition across the United States to the Pacific Ocean. The President wrote a letter to Captain Lewis saying, "The object of your mission is to explore the Missouri river and…the waters of the Pacific ocean whether the Columbia, Oregon, Colorado or any other river may offer the most direct and practicable water communication across the continent for the purpose of commerce." William McGillivray had tried unsuccessfully to interest the British Government in supporting a similar mission.

In 1804, Thompson was brought back to the new company headquarters at Fort William, the former Grand Portage. Here, at the fort named for the superintendent, William McGillivray made Thompson a partner in the NWC. It was a suitable reward for all of David's hard work and loyalty, but he would have preferred being rewarded with more explorations.

Unfortunately, the company sent him back to trade fur in the Muskrat Country. It was a tactical mistake, because the United States Government had sent Lewis and Clark across the continent to find the Pacific. Using Thompson's maps of the Missouri country, Lewis and Clark found the lower part of the Columbia River and followed it to the Pacific in 1805.

Lewis and Clark meeting with natives

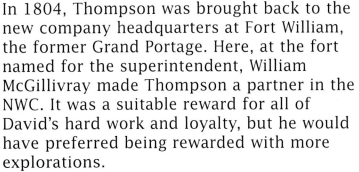

45

A Second Attempt

THE WRONG DIRECTION

When Thompson first came upon the Upper Columbia River, he didn't know it was the Columbia and that the river would take him to the Pacific Ocean. The Columbia River first flows north and away from the ocean before it turns south and winds its way to the Pacific.

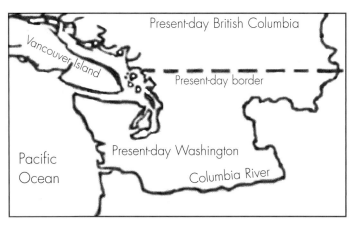

Present-day British Columbia

Vancouver Island

Present-day border

Pacific Ocean

Present-day Washington

Columbia River

McGillivray, without any help from the government, decided to send Thompson west for a second attempt to find a route to the Pacific. This time Thompson was in charge of the expedition. When the Peigans and Blackfoot found out about Thompson's plans, they did everything they could to prevent him and the NWC from trading across the mountains. They wanted to protect their control over trade with the Kootenay and other western tribes.

The natives threatened, harassed and in some cases killed traders. Thompson was unable to escape the native blockade until Captain Lewis unknowingly helped him out. The Lewis and Clark expedition had provoked an attack by the Blackfoot, and some warriors were killed by the American explorers. When the local natives went south to help their brothers fight the Americans, Thompson was finally free to travel across the mountains.

Once over the divide, he found a suitable river and built a trading post on its bank.

A PEACEFUL RELATIONSHIP

Fighting between native people and Europeans was rare in the British-held territory that is now called Canada. Fur traders and Native tribes usually cooperated with each other. It was different in the United States, where U.S. soldiers and native Americans fought many bloody battles.

Under Attack

The Peigans and Blackfoot were angry when they found out that the NWC was trading with the Kootenay. A chief named Old White Swan and his Blackfoot warriors attacked the NWC trading post at Fort Augustus. The natives captured a number of guns and ammunition and threatened more attacks if trading with other tribes continued.

When the Peigans learned Thompson had crossed the mountains, they sent a scouting party to locate him. Thompson, hearing about the attacks, began to build a stockade around his new post. They built three high walls with slots cut in them to fire their guns through when attacked. The back of the fort had no wall, but a steep bank protected them from attack. They could lower a bucket down the bank at night to get fresh water.

By the time a Peigan war party of forty arrived, Thompson and his six men were hiding inside the fort and prepared for battle.

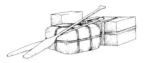

His Protector Saves Him

An early depiction of a native smoking a tobacco pipe

TOBACCO

Tobacco grown by native people was first introduced to Europeans by Sir Walter Raleigh in the 1500s. He returned to England from his voyage to the New World and introduced this strange new custom of smoking tobacco in pipes. It became very popular, and ships began to trade in tobacco between North America and Europe. Hundreds of years later, when European traders travelled west across the continent, they brought tobacco with them. It was one of the most sought-after items among natives. The tobacco trade had come full circle.

Thompson knew the Peigans had held a war council and were determined to destroy his new fort and everyone in it. The only thing that might have held them back temporarily was Thompson's reputation among the Peigan. Many of the warriors had been children when Thompson had first come west to the Peigan camps.

Thompson called a meeting and gave the warriors gifts of tobacco and pipes, asking the young natives to take the gifts back to their Peigan elders at the high council.

Luckily, Kootenae Appee, the old war chief who had sworn to protect David many years ago, was at the council. The old chief persuaded his tribesmen to call off the attack, and the war party returned peacefully back across the mountains.

Three New Trading Posts

MOVING FAST

On one round trip from Kutenai House to Montana, Thompson travelled a thousand kilometres in six weeks. That was a remarkable average of nearly twenty-four kilometres a day over rough and unknown territory. He still found time to fix his position by the stars at night. He carefully recorded his observations in his journal so he could later complete a map of the new territory.

With the threat of attack gone, Thompson began trading with the Kootenay at his new fort. He named the fort Kutenai House. In the following year, 1808, he journeyed south by horseback and canoe into what is now Montana and Idaho. There he built two new trading posts naming them Kullyspell House and Salish House. By the time his expedition returned he had found a pass across the mountains and built three new trading posts. He had established trade with the Kootenay, Salish and Flathead in the fur-rich west. He was still unaware that these were the first trading posts on the Columbia River and its tributaries.

The interior of a Salish longhouse

KOO KOO SINT

At first, natives didn't believe Thompson could find his way by the stars. They knew that knowing the land and remembering the trails told you which direction to travel. By using the stars, however, Thompson showed them he didn't need to follow the old trail home. He could find his way back by any route once he had fixed positions using his sextant. This was a very powerful skill Koo Koo Sint possessed, and his native guides respected him for it.

The Salish-Peigan War

Thompson and his men were not always able to avoid attack. On a trading mission among the Salish, Thompson, with two voyageurs and another fur trader, was ensnared in a gun battle. The Salish, having acquired guns and ammunition from trading with the NWC, went to reclaim buffalo hunting grounds taken from them by the Peigan. Thompson's men were with the Salish when the Peigan attacked.

The fur traders and Salish fired from behind a hastily built barricade at the wild charge of the mounted Peigan warriors. The Salish, outnumbering the Peigan, won the battle. For the Peigan, their worst fears had been realized. Their enemies now had guns from the NWC, and Thompson and his men were to blame. David Thompson, who the Peigan called Koo Koo Sint, meaning the man who looks at stars, was now a hunted man.

50

No Rest

JOHN JACOB ASTOR

CAPITALIST. MANAGER WM. ASTOR ESTATE. NOVELIST. COL. GOV. MORTON'S STAFF (1895-96). FOUNDER ASTOR BAT. U.S.A.

AMERICA'S RICHEST MAN

John Jacob Astor came to America from Germany in 1784 with only pennies in his pocket. By the time he died in 1848, he was the richest man in America. In today's money, he was worth seventy-eight billion dollars. His fortune was started when he formed the American Fur Company in 1808 to trade furs in the Columbia River basin.

Thompson and his men had spent many nights hiding from Peigan war parties. At times the fur traders camped on high ledges above the river to keep safe from attack. They were lucky to escape finally back over the Rockies.

Thompson now looked forward to his long-awaited rest with Charlotte and his children. He was overdue for time off in Montreal and wanted to spend some time with his family. But the NWC had other plans. They instructed Thompson to return immediately to find the Columbia and follow it to the Pacific. The American fur trader John Jacob Astor was threatening to take over the Pacific fur trade by sending ships from the east to build a fort at the mouth of the Columbia River on the Pacific Ocean.

51

No Help

49TH PARALLEL

Later the border along the 49th parallel was extended to form the boundary between the United States and the British territory which became Canada.

The NWC and the Americans were both trying to be first to set up trading posts in the West. There was no border at that time to separate the United States from the British-held territory. Whoever got there first would try to claim the territory around their trading post as their own.

William McGillivray had tried to get the British to send war ships to the Pacific to challenge the Americans, but the British were too busy fighting against Napoleon and the French. The NWC would have to take on Astor and the United States government alone. For this they needed David Thompson.

This Map was made for the North West Company in 1813 -1814 by David Thompson.
"Discovery and Survey of the Oregon Territory to the Pacific Ocean"

Hiding Out

The Peigans were still hunting Thompson, and he feared he would be captured and killed. At one point he had to spend many days alone and out of sight in a hidden camp near the Brazeau River. Suffering in the cold and snow and weak with hunger, he finally made his way back to the NWC post at Rocky Mountain House. Rocky Mountain House soon became surrounded by tents as Peigan, Blood and Sarcee tribesmen gathered to harass traders and prevent Thompson from leaving. Some chiefs wanted to attack the trading post, but once again Kootenae Appee was able to keep them from doing so. Nevertheless, Thompson, with twenty-four men and the same number of horses, had to wait for his opportunity to slip past the blockade.

It wasn't until many months later, in October of 1810 that he made his escape. This time he didn't travel by the usual route but headed north to avoid any pursuers. He was also going to attempt the unthinkable; crossing the mountains in winter.

Rocky Mountain House

ROCKY MOUNTAIN HOUSE

Rocky Mountain House, in present day Alberta, was a main headquarters for the NWC in the West. Today it is a National Historic Site with many displays about David Thompson and the fur trade.

KOOTENAE APPEE

No one knows how Kootenae Appee died, but the famous Peigan war chief kept his promise to protect David Thompson. At least twice, Kootenae Appee saved Thompson from harm. Thompson held the chief in great respect.

Crossing the Rockies in Winter

ATHABASKA PASS

The Athabaska Pass was to become the main trading route followed for generations. The NWC and later the HBC hauled fortunes in furs across the pass Thompson had discovered.

David Thompson in the Athabaska Pass

Crossing the Rocky Mountains in mid-winter would be one of the hardest things Thompson and his men had ever done. Even some voyageurs, whose ability to take the hardships of the trail were legendary, began to leave for home. But Thompson pressed higher into the mountains and slogged through even deeper snow.

Eventually his horses could go no further and some were killed for food. The others were exchanged for dogs and sleds. More men deserted as the temperature fell to -34° Celsius near the ice-clad peaks.

Then, with only half of his men and a few dog sleds left, a miracle of nature saved his expedition. A Chinook wind, which sometimes blows across the mountains, warmed the winter air to 0°Celsius. Thompson and his men were then able to safely cross the 1,500 metre summit of the Athabaska Pass.

More Delays

FORT ASTOR BECOMES A NWC POST AFTER ALL

David Thompson may not have been the first to the mouth of the Columbia, but he was the first to trace and map the river's entire route. Even though the Americans built the first post at the mouth of the river, Fort Astor was later taken over by the NWC. In 1812, a war broke out between Canada and the United States. Jacob Astor was worried his new fur trading post would be lost to the British so he sold the post to the NWC.

Thompson's men and supplies were so depleted that he could not continue without finding more men and provisions. In April of 1811, he headed for his old trading post at Salish House. Spring travel in wet snow and across half-frozen lakes was slow.

Finally, by July 3, he had re-supplied, built a boat, and was heading for the mouth of the Columbia. Twelve days later, on July 15, 1811, his boat reached the Pacific Ocean. There, at the mouth of the river, a pole was flying the American flag and behind that were some log huts. It was a small fur trading settlement called Fort Astor. Jacob Astor's ship had arrived first.

Fort Astor

His Mission Accomplished

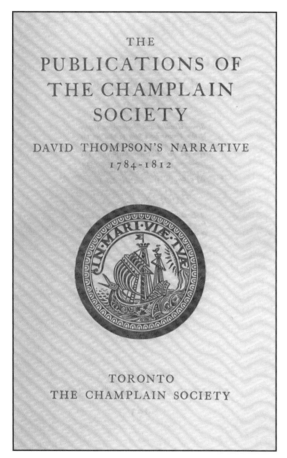

THE
PUBLICATIONS OF
THE CHAMPLAIN
SOCIETY

DAVID THOMPSON'S NARRATIVE
1784-1812

IN·MARI·VIÆ·TVÆ

TORONTO
THE CHAMPLAIN SOCIETY

David Thompson's writings were found and published many years after his death by Joseph Tyrell and the Champlain Society

David Thompson did the only thing he could do. He set up trading posts to compete with Americans, and he mapped the new route he had found. Although it may have seemed like failure at that moment, it was an amazing accomplishment. He had found the trading route to the Pacific that both Simon Fraser and Alexander MacKenzie had tried so hard to find but had failed.

Thompson had single-handedly surveyed a continental area whose scale is unparalleled in human history.

When Thompson retired from the fur trade, he moved with his family to Terrebonne near Montreal in 1812 to finish his map of the west.

His Final Years

Three years later, in 1815, Thompson moved to Glengarry County, Ontario. There he worked for the next ten years mostly surveying the Canadian border for the Boundary Commission.

In 1826, he found work surveying canals, townships and land grants while working to complete his great map of the west. By 1843, the map of Canada from Hudson Bay to the Pacific was completed, using the observations he had taken on his travels. The map covered an area of 3.9 million square kilometres.

It wasn't until late in his life, at age seventy-three, that he began writing his narrative. By that time his eyesight was failing, and he had lost almost all of his savings through poor investments or loans to his children. For his remaining years, he struggled to complete his narrative and find a publisher.

He died penniless and unknown in 1857 at the age of eighty-six, never having completed his final task. His unfinished manuscript was discovered and published in 1915, almost sixty years after his death.

The World's Greatest Land Geographer

THANKS TO JOSEPH TYRELL

If it had not been for Joseph Tyrell, David Thompson might have remained unknown. Like other later explorers, Tyrell used Thompson's forgotten journals and maps to help plan new surveys and explorations. Working for the Canadian government in the late 1800s, the geologist became famous for the important discovery of dinosaur skeletons and huge coal deposits in Alberta. His exploration and mapping of large unknown areas in northern Saskatchewan and Manitoba were reported in newspapers and scientific journals, and he received many awards during his lifetime. Perhaps nobody knew better than Tyrell how much David Thompson had been overlooked.

In 1927, the geologist Joseph T. Tyrell erected a column crowned with a sextant over Thompson's neglected grave. It was the first time anyone had brought public attention to the great explorer's resting place. Tyrell edited Thompson's journals and maps, which the geologist had so carefully studied and used over the years. He had them published by the Champlain Society in 1916 in a final act of appreciation.

Today David Thompson is becoming recognized as the world's greatest land geographer. His achievements are being commemorated in museums and science centres throughout Canada and the United States. Highways are now named after him, complete with sign boards erected in his honour. There are plans to rename mountains to pay tribute to his enormous contribution to Canada. He is finally taking his rightful place in Canadian and world history. In the words taken from the small monument over his grave, he is the "GREATEST OF CANADIAN GEOGRAPHERS."

David Thompson's greatest achievement, his map of the west

David Thompson's life and times

1770   David Thompson is born in London, England, to a poor family.

1777   Because of his father's death five years earlier, Thompson is sent to Grey Coat Charity School for the poor, where he learns mathematics and navigation.

1784   Leaves Grey Coat School and embarks on a ship for Rupert's Land as an apprentice to the Hudson's Bay Company.

1785   Transferred from Churchill to York Factory.

1787   Journeys inland to build South Branch House and winters with the Peigans, natives of the Plains.

1789   Recovering from his broken leg, Thompson meets Philip Turnor, who teaches him how to survey and make maps.

1790-96   Stays on with HBC after apprenticeship is completed to work as trader and surveyor.

1797   Thompson completes his service with the HBC and joins the rival North West Company.

1798   Makes survey and mapping expeditions to the headwaters of the Mississippi and Missouri Rivers, visits Mandan villages and returns to survey Lake Superior.

1799   Marries Charlotte Small, the thirteen-year-old half-native daughter of a fur trader. They remain married for the rest of their lives.

1800-06   Surveys Peace River and Lake Athabasca, becomes partner in NWC. Turns attention to crossing the Rocky Mountains from Rocky Mountain House.

1807-10	Crosses Rocky Mountains. Trades and sets up posts in what are now British Columbia, Montana and Idaho. Opposed by the Peigans, he searches for another pass.
1811	Crosses Athabaska Pass in winter to avoid resistance from the Peigans. Travels the Columbia River from headwaters to the Pacific to find Americans already at the river's mouth.
1812	Leaves fur trading and returns with his family to live near Montreal.
1814-25	Lives and works in Ontario.
1814-43	Finishes his maps of the Northwest. Works as a surveyor and helps map Canada-U.S. border.
1843-50	Lives in poverty and suffers near blindness. Begins writing about his travels.
1857	Dies at age eighty-six without finishing his writing. His wife Charlotte dies three months later. Both are buried in unmarked graves in Montreal.
1914	His writings are discovered by Joseph Tyrell and published in 1916.
2006	The David Thompson North American Bicentennial is established to commemorate his life and achievements.

About the Author

Tom Shardlow holds a B.Sc. and M.Sc. from the University of British Columbia and is a research biologist with more than thirty articles contributed to international scientific and technical journals. His diverse writing ranges from poetry and prize- winning short fiction published in literary magazines to book reviews for *Quill and Quire* and *Canadian Geographic.* His freelance work, which includes creative drawings and photographs, often appears as feature articles in magazines and in newspapers. Tom has completed a biography of David Thompson, *A Trail by Stars*, and is currently working on a popular history of biology and a science fiction novel. He lives with his family on Vancouver Island.

Acknowledgements

The author is indebted to Barbara Belyea, David Malaher and John Wilson for sharing their knowledge and research.

Some Terms Explained

Almanac: a book that contains astronomical or meteorological data arranged according to months, weeks and days of the year.

Apprenticeship: training in a craft or occupation. This training is given on the job. In the past, apprentices often lived with their instructor.

Contraband: illegally traded (smuggled) goods such as food or tobacco.

Epitaph: an inscription on a tombstone in honour of the deceased person.

Factory: a trading post in a foreign land.

Geology: the scientific study of the history, origin and structure of the planet.

Headwaters: the source of a river. Many rivers start from streams in mountains, and they drain into oceans or lakes.

Latitude: the angular distance north or south of the earth's equator, which is measured in degrees.

Longitude: the angular distance on the earth's surface, measured east or west from the prime meridian at Greenwich, England, to the meridian passing through a position, expressed in degrees (or hours), minutes and seconds.

Métis: a person of mixed French-Canadian and native ancestry.

Midshipman: a temporary rank held by young naval officers.

Orphanage: a home for children whose parents have either died or abandoned them.

Sextant: a navigational instrument that measures the altitudes of celestial bodies to determine latitude and longitude, using a 60° measurement.

Pass: a gap in mountains that allows easy passage through them.

Pemmican: a traditional native food, good for taking on journeys, made of dried fruit and meat.

Portage: travelling with a canoe between bodies of water. Canoes have to be carried for a distance between lakes or rivers.

Surveying: determining the boundaries, area or elevations (on the earth's surface) by measuring angles and distances.

Trading post: an establishment where groups meet to trade goods, such as furs, food, tobacco and alcohol.

Tributary: a smaller stream that flows into a larger river.

Resources that were used in writing this book

BOOKS:

Columbia Journals: David Thompson by Barbara Belyea (ed.) (Montreal and Kingston: McGill-Queen's University Press, 1994)

The Nor'Westers: The Fight for the Fur Trade by Marjorie Wilkins Campbell (Toronto: Macmillan, 1974)

David Thompson's Travels in Western North America, 1784-1812 by Victor G. Hopwood (ed.) (Toronto: MacMillan, 1971)

The Well-Dressed Explorer by J. Gottfred (Northwest Journal, Volume IV, 21 – 24, Retrieved November 7, 2002 http://www.northwestjournal.ca/sample.html, 2002)

Epic Wanderer: David Thompson and the Mapping of the Canadian West by D'Arcy Jenish (Toronto: Doubleday, 2003)

David Thompson: Fur trader, explorer, geographer by James K. Smith (Toronto: Oxford University Press, 1971)

David Thompson's Instruments and Methods in the Northwest, 1790-1812 by David Smith (Cartographica, 18, (4), 1-17. 1981)

David Thompson's Surveys of the Missouri/Mississippi Territory in 1797-98 by David Malaher (Paper presented to the 9th North American Fur Trade Conference & Rupert's Land Colloquium. University of Missouri at St Louis, Missouri, 2006)

WEBSITES:

David Thompson Bicentennials Partnership
www.davidthompson200.ca

Pathfinders and Passageways
An informative website devoted to the history of exploration of Canada. Contains some information about David Thompson
http://www.collectionscanada.ca/explorers

Index

Photo and Art Credits

Illustrations by Chrissie Wysotski
Cover illustration, pages a4, 5, 10, 12, 24, 27, 33, 38, 44, 47, 50, 57

Library and Archives Canada
Pages 2: C-010645, Acc. No. 1979-82-3, Source: Galerie Bernard Desroches, Montréal, Québec, 3: C-069934, Acc. No. 1972-26-572, 7: C-082981, 8: Prince Rupert C-027585, Prince Rupert reading charter C-013958, Acc. No. 1991-35-24, 11: C-041716, Acc. No. 1970-188-843, W.H. Coverdale Collection of Canadiana, 13: C-040185, Acc. No. 1970-188-1961, W.H. Coverdale Collection of Canadiana, 14: e02291340, Acc. No. R9266-624, Peter Winkworth Collection of Canadiana, 15: Hearne portrait C-020053, Hearne on journey C-070250, Acc. No. 1972-26-1386, artist C.W. Jefferys, 16: C-000164, Acc. No. 1956-6-1, 17: C-002774, Acc. No. 1989-401-2, artist Frances Anne Hopkins, 18: C-008373, Acc. No. 1934-380-1, 19: C-073663, Acc. No. 1972-26-777, artist C.W. Jefferys, 20: C-001875, O.B. Buell, 21: C-010502, Acc. No. 1989-492-2, 23: C-000439, Acc. No. 1946-146-1, Gift of Mrs. J.B. Jardine, 25: C-038951, artist Robert Hood, 26: C-100027, Acc. No. 1989-292-4, artist George Catlin, 28: C-108129, 30: C-073573, Acc. No. 1972-26-1406, artist C.W. Jefferys, 34: NWC coat of arms, C-008711, Acc. No. 1957-101, 35: nlc000716, 36: C-000977, artist Col. J. Bouchette, 37: C-000167, 39: NMC 51713, 40: C-001075, Acc. No. 1950-63-9, 41: C-035952, Acc. No. 1968-115-1, 42: nlc000725, 43: PA-031616, Albertype Company, 48: C-040363, Acc. No. 1970-188-1048, W.H. Coverdale Collection of Canadiana, 49: C-150725, Acc. No. R9266-343, Peter Winkworth Collection of Canadiana, artist Edward M. Richardson, 53: PA-038031, Geological Survey of Canada, 54: C-070258, Acc. No. 1972-26-9, artist C.W. Jefferys, 56: nlc000724

Archives of Ontario
59: Map of the North-west Territory of the Province of Canada by David Thompson (1770-1857). [1814] F 443, R-C(U), AO 1541.
David Thompson fonds

Toronto Reference Library
Page 34: HBC Coat of Arms, J. Ross Robertson Collection, T16985

Reprinted with the permission of the Champlain Society
Page 52